**NAILED IT!**

Extreme

# CAVE
# DIVING

Virginia Loh-Hagan

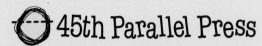
# 45th Parallel Press

Published in the United States of America by Cherry Lake Publishing
Ann Arbor, Michigan
www.cherrylakepublishing.com

Content Adviser: Liv Williams, Editor, www.iLivExtreme.com
Reading Adviser: Marla Conn, ReadAbility, Inc.
Photo Credits: ©Adnan Buyuk/Shutterstock.com, cover, 1; ©Octavio Jones/ZUMA Press/Newscom, 5; ©Soren Egeberg
Photography/Shutterstock.com, 6; ©think4photop/Shutterstock.com, 8; ©Durden Images/Shutterstock.com, 11; ©salajean/
Shutterstock.com, 12; ©aquapix/Shutterstock.com, 15; ©gameover2012/istockphoto.com, 17; ©Wiktor Bubniak/Shutterstock.
com, 19; ©mollypix/istockphoto.com, 21; ©pniesen/Thinkstock.com, 22; ©nudiblue/Shutterstock.com, 25; ©Paul Vinten/
Shutterstock.com, 27; ©iurii/Shutterstock.com, 28; ©Trusjom/Shutterstock.com, multiple interior pages; ©Kues/Shutterstock.
com, multiple interior pages

**45th Parallel Press** is an imprint of Cherry Lake Publishing.

Library of Congress Cataloging-in-Publication Data

Loh-Hagan, Virginia.
  Extreme cave diving / by Virginia Loh-Hagan.
    pages cm. -- (Nailed it!)
  Includes bibliographical references and index.
  ISBN 978-1-63470-490-8 (hardcover) -- ISBN 978-1-63470-550-9 (pdf) -- ISBN 978-1-63470-610-0 (paperback) --
ISBN 978-1-63470-670-4 (ebook)
  1. Cave diving. 2. Extreme sports. I. Title.
  GV200.63.L64 2016
  796.52'5--dc23
                                      2015026820

## ABOUT THE AUTHOR

Dr. Virginia Loh-Hagan is an author, university professor, former classroom teacher, and curriculum designer. The only thing she wants to dive into is a bowl of crab dip. She lives in San Diego with her very tall husband and very naughty dogs. To learn more about her, visit www.virginialoh.com.

# Table of Contents

# The Most Dangerous Sport in the World

*Who is Judi Bedard? Who is Jill Heinerth?*
*Who is Brian Kakuk?*

Judi Bedard dived 130 feet (39.6 meters) into the water. She scouted an underwater cave. Something was wrong with her gas tank. She was brought to the surface. She wasn't breathing. She didn't have a heartbeat. Blood gushed from her eyes and ears.

Bedard was **cave diving** in Eagle Nest Sink. It's in Florida. Cave diving is diving into underwater caves. Some think it's the most dangerous sport in the world. A sign at Eagle Nest Sink reads, "Stop. Prevent your death. Go no farther."

Bedard did not wake up for two months. She got better. She trained. She dived again. She explored underwater caves again. She said, "It's like heaven on Earth … I'm **undaunted**." Undaunted means she's not afraid.

Jill Heinerth is not afraid. Most people are scared of underwater caves. But she isn't. She said, "As a cave diver, I swim through the veins of Mother Earth."

Eagle Nest Sink is the "Grand Canyon" of cave diving.

CAVE DIVING IN THIS AREA IS EXTREMELY DANGEROUS - EVEN LIFE THREATENING! DO NOT DIVE UNLESS YOU ARE A CERTIFIED CAVE DIVER !!

Cave divers dive in extreme locations.

She also dives in icebergs. She was in ice-cold water for three hours. She got back to the surface. She couldn't get out of the water. The iceberg was melting. Water poured down from it. She said, "There was a possibility we weren't going to get out."

She didn't want to get trapped. She jammed her fingers in holes in the iceberg. She climbed up. Two hours later, the iceberg fell apart. It became a pile of slush. She felt lucky to be alive.

Brian Kakuk completed more than 3,000 cave dives. He explores underwater caves in the Bahamas. He's done this for over 20 years. He guides cave divers. He takes them to amazing places. He makes sure people are safe.

NAILED IT!

## Spotlight Biography: Evan Bozanic

Evan Bozanic is the youngest person to dive all seven continents. He set the record in Bushman's Cave. It's in South Africa. Several cave divers have died there. He did this before his 15th birthday. At age 11, he became the world's youngest person to dive in Antarctica. At age 12, he created his own diving equipment for a science fair project. He is passionate about diving. He said, "My immediate project is finishing the book I'm writing about my record dives. Besides just setting the record, I want to tell people about what I saw in each place, especially environmental changes." Bozanic loves exploring. He said, "My favorite destination is somewhere no one has been before."

Cave divers have a lot of diving experience. Brian Kakuk was a U.S. Navy diver for seven years.

Kakuk swims through black water. He goes down slowly. He follows cave walls. He moves his lamp forward. He collects water samples. He points to a blind fish. He spots things most divers don't see. He's discovered more than 12 new animals. He's found human bones.

"He spots things most divers don't see."

# Lifesaving Skills and Equipment

*What are the three main types of diving? What is cave diving? What are special skills that cave divers need? Why is teamwork important? What types of cave-diving equipment are needed?*

There are three main types of diving. **Open-water** diving is the first level. It's easy to get back to the surface. Divers just swim up. They can see sunlight.

**Cavern** diving is the next level. Caverns are the areas before caves. Divers can see the entrance. They can see sunlight.

Cave diving is the scariest level. Cave divers dive more than 130 feet (39.6 m) down. They can't see sunlight. Divers can't see the surface. They are enclosed by the cave.

They dive into blackness. They dive into tight spaces.

Cave divers take classes for several years. They learn to use gear. They practice diving.

They have a special swimming style. They look for cracks. They grab hold with their fingertips. They pull and let go. They glide through the cave.

Caverns, caves, and shipwrecks are called overhead environments. There is a barrier between the diver and the surface.

Cave diving is high risk. Cave divers need a lot of special skills and gear.

Cave divers depend on their teams. Viktor Lyagushkin explored underwater caves in Russia. He said, "We do control our risks. Before each dive, we discuss each moment to find a solution to any situation we are faced with. If it is too risky, we do not dive. We must be aware of each step. Or you will die."

Cave divers carry more gear than open water divers. They carry twice as much gear. They carry backup supplies.

They have **scuba** gear. This gear helps divers breathe underwater. Gas tanks have special gas mixes. The divers wear masks and hoods. They wear suits. This gear keeps them warm.

## Advice from the Field: Pascal Bernabé

Pascal Bernabé has a world record. He dived 1,083 feet (330 m). He started diving at age 19. He describes cave diving as being in space. He said, "It's very quiet. It's like being on the moon." Bernabé advises cave divers to adapt. This means they have to be willing to change. He said, "There are several kinds of caves: small, big, narrow. And you adapt yourself and your equipment to each cave. You put your tanks behind you, next to you, or you push them forward, depending on the size of the cave. You have to adapt yourself to each situation."

Cave divers worry about getting lost. They have **navigation** gear. This helps them find their way. They use **guide lines**. They tie ropes in certain places. These ropes guide them in and out of caves.

They work in darkness. They bring special lights. **Silt** covers most cave floors. Silt is soft dirt. It's easily stirred up. It covers diving lights. It's hard to see.

The average cave dive is about one hour. Some can last 15 hours.

# From Cousteau to Conservation

*What was the first recorded cave dive? Who is Jacques-Yves Cousteau? Who is Sheck Exley? How did cave diving develop?*

The first recorded cave dive was in France. It was in 1878. Nello Ottonelli dived 75 feet (23 m). He wore a large helmet. He wore heavy boots. He got air through tubes. Air came from a pump at the water's surface.

Jacques-Yves Cousteau was the first scuba cave diver. He introduced the Aqua-Lung in 1943. It was a diving suit.

In the 1970s, cave diving became popular. People cave dived without training. Many people died. Florida wanted to ban cave diving. But groups organized. They created training programs.

Sheck Exley developed the sport. He created safety rules. He was the first to explore underwater caves. He was the first to dive over 1,000 caves. He cave dived for more than 29 years. He made over 4,000 cave dives. He was the first to dive below 800 feet (244 m).

Since the 1980s, improvements have been made. The gear is safer and more advanced. **Scooters** help cave divers swim faster. Scooters are like backpack **jets**. Cave divers

In the past, cave divers didn't have the gear they have today.

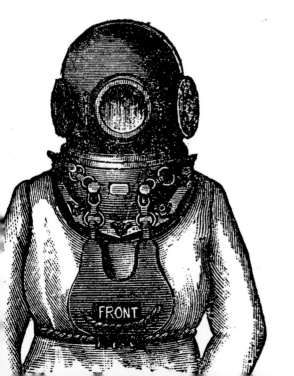

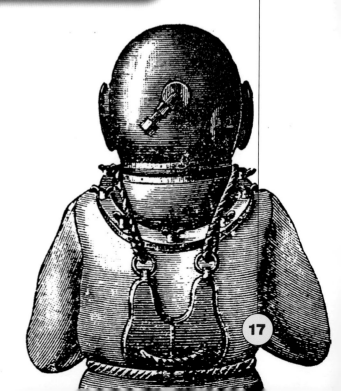

# Extreme Cave Diving: Know the Lingo

**Braille dive:** a dive where you can't see very well; divers have to feel their way around

**Bug:** lobster

**Call the dive:** giving a thumbs-up command to finish the dive

**Caver:** cave diver

**Coffin cave:** a cave used as a burial site

**Feed the fish:** vomit or throw up

**Get wet:** go diving

**Milky:** water that has a white tint

**Skip breathing:** holding breath to save air

**Sneak dive:** a dive into an area where you do not have permission

**Spelunking:** exploring caves, not underwater

**Stroke:** a diver with an unsafe attitude

**Sump:** a point in the cave passage when the water meets the roof

**The bends:** decompression sickness

**Twilight zone:** deeper than 200 feet (61 m) in the ocean

More than 95 percent of cave-diving deaths happened because divers were untrained.

swim about 50 feet (15 m) per minute. Scooters help them swim three times faster. Cave divers can cover large distances and save air.

Today, cave divers focus on exploration. They focus on **conservation**. Conservation means protecting nature.

# Dangers of Cave Diving

*What are the dangers of cave diving?*

Training and gear are expensive. Cave divers could die. They could drown. They could get **decompression** sickness. Decompression is the lowering of pressure. Human bodies can't handle low depths. Going down and coming up too fast are dangerous. It creates bubbles in the blood.

Cave divers can't just go up to the surface. First, they have to swim back. They have to get out of the cave. Caves are like mazes. Cave divers could get lost. They could get trapped. They only have so much air. In caves, water flows in strong currents. Cave divers could get pulled in.

Cave divers depend on their gear. Bad gear is deadly. Not having enough supplies is deadly. John Robinson Jr. died while cave diving. People believe he ran out of air.

Craig Simon cave dived at Eagle Nest Sink. He didn't come up. Two days later, rescue cave divers found him. His body was tangled in guide lines. People believe he left to check out another tunnel. He may have kicked up silt. He lost his way.

Decompression sickness causes joint pain, heart attacks, or ruptured blood vessels. Ruptured means exploded.

Cave divers know the risks. They still want to go cave diving.

Cave divers have no room to make mistakes. Dirk Bennett and Ben Perkins know this. They explored the Bennett Spring caves. They swam 1,700 feet (518 m). They swam through tight tunnels. They trained for weeks. They reached the safe limit on their tanks. So they turned back.

They followed the guide lines. Chris Hill watched them from the top. He had extra supplies. They took no chances.

## When Extreme Is Too Extreme!

Ahmed Gabr dived 1,066 feet (325 m). This is deeper than three football fields. He dived into the Red Sea. It's in the Middle East. He set a world record for the world's deepest male scuba dive. It took him 12 minutes to dive down. It took him 14 hours to get back to the surface. Returning too quickly is risky. He didn't want to die or get sick. He had nine tanks. He hung on to a special rope. Gabr wanted to prove that humans can survive deep-sea conditions. He'd been training for four years. To add to the danger, he had a special guest. A baby white tip oceanic shark followed him. He posted on Facebook, "Had a baby shark for 6 hours around me. We kept each other busy."

# Cave Explorers and Astronauts

*How are cave divers like explorers? How are they like astronauts?*

Cave divers are explorers. Underwater caves have a lot to offer scientists. Scientists aren't trained to go there. So they need cave divers.

A team of cave divers found an underwater graveyard. They were in Madagascar. They dived down 82 feet (25 m). They found hundreds of animal **fossils**. Fossils are preserved plants or animal bones. Scientists learn a lot from these caves.

Another team cave dived in Spain. They spent 50 hours

underwater. They camped deep underground. A team member said, "It's an incredible buzz to explore farther than anyone has been ever before."

Brett Hemphill cave dived into Weeki Wachee. It's in Florida. It's a **spring**. A spring is a source of water coming from the ground.

Fewer than 10 percent of the known underwater caves in the world have been explored.

Hemphill held his tanks in his hand. He dived in. He was crammed deep in a hole. His head barely fit through. He grabbed a rock. He pulled himself forward. He discovered a new underwater cave. He said, "It's not about claiming it in your name or saying you're the first person. But I really enjoy bringing that information back to the people."

Hemphill thinks he's an underwater **astronaut**. Astronauts travel to space. He wants to build an underwater space station.

Matt Vinzant is a cave diver. He said, "It's one of the coolest feelings ever … to go somewhere no one has ever been. More people have been on the moon than where we are going today …"

"He discovered a new underwater cave."

Exploring caves is called caving, potholing, or spelunking. Studying caves is called speleology.

Cave diving is like floating in space. Space and caves are both unexplored territories.

Cave diving may become part of space training. The program is called CAVES. It stands for Cooperative Adventure for Valuing and Exercising Skills. Astronauts spend a week underground. They pretend to be on a real space mission.

Space travel and cave diving are alike. There's much danger. There are great rewards.

# That Happened?!?

Alejandro Alvarez's hobby is cave diving. He and some friends cave dived into the Black Hole. It's in Mexico's Yucatan Peninsula. He went deeper and deeper. He swam into a tunnel. Suddenly, the floor disappeared! He said, "It was immensely dark. We had to follow along the wall. ... Then, I could see something floating." He saw a leg bone. It was of an ancient elephant-like animal. He cave dived for several weeks. He saw a girl's skull. It was resting on a ledge. It had a full set of teeth. It was a 12,000-year-old skeleton. It's of a teenager. Scientists believe she fell into the hole before water filled the caves. It's the hemisphere's oldest and most complete skeleton. It tells scientists a lot about how American humans developed. Alvarez said, "We immediately realized the importance. It was very exciting."

# Did You Know?

- *Sanctum* is a movie. It was inspired by a real cave-diving story. In 1988, 13 cave divers got trapped. They were in Australia. A storm caved in the entrance.

- Agnes Milowka worked on *Sanctum*. She was the stunt double in the drowning scene. In real life, she later drowned during a cave dive. She ran out of air. Her death was similar to the movie story. She forgot her spare tank. She was trapped in a small space.

- Troglobites are insects. They live in the dark parts of caves. They don't have color. They have no eyes. They can go weeks or months without food. They can live for more than 100 years.

- Pascal Bernabé cave dived for close to 9 hours. He ate through a tube. He ate milk mixed with sugar. He ate cream, mashed potatoes, and soup. He read books. He listened to music.

- Tom Iliffe has explored more than 1,500 underwater caves. He's discovered over 300 forms of marine life.

- Mammoth Cave National Park is the longest known cave system in the world. It's in Kentucky.

- Voronya Cave is the deepest known cave. It's in the country of Georgia. It's 7,208 feet (2,197 m) deep.

- Brett Hemphill caught a wild alligator. It was in the way of a cave entrance.

# Consider This!

TAKE A POSITION! The National Speleological Society states, "A well-equipped, educated and prudent cave diver has more to worry about driving to the dive site and walking to the water than what happens during the dive." What does this quote mean? Do you agree or disagree? Argue your point with reasons and evidence.

SAY WHAT? There are three different types of diving. Explain each type. Explain the differences and similarities between cavern diving and cave diving.

THINK ABOUT IT! Diving at high pressures underwater is risky. Think about a soda bottle. When you shake a soda bottle, some bubbles go to the surface. If you quickly open up the cap, the liquid will burst out. Fizzy gas rises to the top. How can you keep this from happening? How is this like cave diving?

SEE A DIFFERENT SIDE! Some people believe cave diving should be banned. They're not concerned about safety. They're concerned about conservation. They want to protect underwater caves from humans. Research this viewpoint. What do you think about it?

# Learn More: Resources

## PRIMARY SOURCES

*Extreme Cave Diving*, a PBS documentary (NOVA, season 37, episode 13; June 19, 2013), http://www.pbs.org/wgbh/nova/earth/extreme-cave-diving.html.

## SECONDARY SOURCES

Bailer, Darice. Dive: *Your Guide to Snorkeling, Scuba, Night-Diving, Freediving, Exploring Shipwrecks, Caves, and More*. Washington, DC: National Geographic Extreme Sports, 2008.

Covert, Kim. *Extreme Diving*. Mankato, MN: Capstone Press, 2005.

## WEB SITES

National Association for Cave Diving: http://www.nacdmembers.com/

National Speleological Society Cave Diving Section: http://www.nsscds.org

Professional Scuba Association International: http://www.psai.com

# Glossary

**astronaut** (AS-truh-nawt) a trained person who travels to space

**cave diving** (KAVE DIVE-eng) diving to underwater caves

**cavern** (KAV-ern) the area before a cave; the entryway to a cave

**conservation** (kahn-sur-VAY-shuhn) protecting nature

**decompression** (de-kuhm-PRESH-uhn) reduction in air pressure

**fossils** (FAH-suhlz) preserved plants or animal bones

**guide lines** (GIDE LYNZ) ropes that help divers move in and out of caves

**jets** (JETZ) a forceful stream of water or gas

**navigation** (nav-ih-GAY-shun) finding one's way

**open-water** (OH-puhn WAW-tur) having easy access to the surface

**scooters** (SKOO-turz) backpack jets that help divers swim faster

**scuba** (SKOO-buh) self-contained underwater breathing apparatus; underwater breathing equipment

**silt** (SILT) dirt and sand at the bottom of the ocean floor

**spring** (SPRING) a source of water coming from the ground

**undaunted** (uhn-DAWN-tid) not afraid to continue doing something

# Index